Magic Book of Spells
Alexis Morrigan

Money, Wealth, and Fortune Spells

Career and Job Spells

Household Spells of All Types

Love Attraction Spells

Relationship and Marriage Spells

Fertility Spells

Good Luck Spells

Power Spells

Peace Spells

Banishing Spells

Defense Spells

Dream Spells

Energy Spells

Enchantment Spells

Protection Spells

Introduction

The spells in this book give exact casting instructions. That being said, each spell you consider casting needs to feel right to you. Don't cast anything or follow any instruction that gives you a bad feeling or that just feels wrong to you. These spells are guidelines, and you should always follow your own mind first. If you feel a particular spell would be better with a different color candle, or even different wording, go ahead and make the substitution.

General Candle Color Correspondence

White: White represents balance and is the lunar color. It can be substituted for any other color. It represents cleansing, clairvoyance, healing, and enlightenment.

Silver: Silver represents the moon Goddess, reincarnation, the removal of negative energy, stability, and intuition.

Red: Red represents Aries and Scorpio, love, health, passion, fertility, willpower, strength, courage, sexuality, determination, and increases magnetism in spell work.

Pink: Pink represents love, fertility, romance, femininity, friendship, emotional love, healing, peace, and honor.

Magenta: Magenta is used to hasten results.

Orange: Orange is a solar color and represents Leo, creativity, confidence, ambition, legal or business success, kindness, encouragement, and good luck.

Yellow: Yellow is a solar color and represents vitality, change, progress, safe travel, an increase in learning abilities and mental prowess, energy, and also helps with visualization and the creative process.

Gold: Gold represents the sun deities, solar energy, general financial success, success with investments, world power, luxury, will increase your ability to overcome obstacles, and can attract cosmic energy.

Green: Green represents the Goddess, money, prosperity, wealth, nature, fertility, animals, peace and peace in your home.

Blue: Blue represents sea or sky deities, truth, wisdom, bravery, courage, calmness, honor, harmony, and can cause prophetic dreams to increase or become clear.

Purple: Purple represents Saturn and the elements, counteracts negativity and black magic, reverses curses, and increases psychic and meditative power.

Brown: Brown represents the earth and earthly beings, material increase, and attracts lost objects.

Gray: Gray is used to cancel out negativity, and for complex meditation and visualization.

Black: Black represents the deities of the underworld and Saturn. It is used to repel or to banish negativity, and to free yourself of bad habits.

Days of the Week

Sunday:

Colors: Yellow, orange, or gold
Deities: Sun
Element: Fire
Spells: Beauty, friendship, healing, creativity, authority, achievement, success, and goals

Monday:

Colors: Silver or white
Deities: Moon
Element: Water
Spells: Home and family life, healing, intuition, and growth

Tuesday:

Colors: Red or orange
Deities: Mars
Element: Fire
Spells: Courage, intellect, strength, discipline, enemies, and conflict

Wednesday:

Colors: Purple
Deities: Mercury
Element: Earth
Spells: Career, communication, travel, finance, intelligence, legal matters, and general luck

Thursday:

Colors: Green or royal blue
Deities: Jupiter
Element: Fire
Spells: Honor, family, loyalty, faithfulness, and prosperity

Friday:

Colors: Pink or aqua
Deities: Venus

Element: Air
Spells: Love, romance, fertility, luxury, art, harmony

Saturday:

Colors: Black or dark purple
Deities: Saturn
Element: Earth
Spells: Creativity, hope, change, and removes negativity

Phases of the Moon

New Moon: New beginnings, transformations, health, love, romance and hope

Waxing Moon: Accomplishments, growth, success, health, creativity, and learning

Full Moon: Manifesting, sexuality, protection, legal work, finances, and achievements

Waning Moon: Cleansing, releasing, and banishing

Dark Moon: Resting and peace

Simple Candle Spell to Bring Money

You will need:

3 green candles
3 shining coins (any denomination)

Instructions:

Arrange the 3 candles on your altar like a triangle. Each candle should be one point of the triangle.

Light the candles starting at the top point and moving clockwise.

Lay your 3 shining coins inside the boundaries of the triangle.

Say the following 3 times:

Goddess of the Moon
I ask you for a boon
Grant me silver, grant me gold
Grant me more than my hands can hold
As I will it, so mote it be

Snuff out your candles, starting with the top candle and moving clockwise. The 3 shining coins should be carried in your purse or pocket (or anywhere on your person) for 3 days following this spell.

Spell for a Powerful Necklace to Attract Money

You will need:

Necklace of green stones or crystals (It is very important you like this necklace and it is attractive to you.)
Small white cloth bag
Minimum 6 inches of gold thread
Consecrated water
Coin (any denomination)
Full moon

Instructions:

Take your green necklace and sprinkle a few drops of consecrated water on it.

Place it in the cloth bag along with your coin, and bind the bag shut with gold thread.

Bury the cloth bag outside during a full moon. Then say the following:

Goddess, hear my plea
Let my money increase
Let me live in financial peace
Let the money flow towards me, as easy as can be
As I will it, so mote it be

Leave the area. Every night you must go to the spot where the cloth bag is buried and repeat the chant. Your mind must be calm and focused while you do this. If it is not calm and focused take a few minutes before you visit the area to get in the right mindset.

At the beginning of the next full moon, dig up the cloth bag.

Remove the necklace and clean any debris off with consecrated water.

Immediately wear the necklace.

Take the cloth bag and gold thread and burn them over the dug up hole.

The coin and ashes should be buried there.

Continue to wear your necklace as often as you can to give this spell strength.

Knotted Rope Money Spell

<u>You will need</u>:

White cord or ribbon 3 feet in length
Nighttime

<u>Instructions</u>:

After midnight on any night, take your cord and say the chant below, with each line tie a knot into the cord until you have 9 knots. These are the words you say as each knot is formed:

With knot of one the spells begun
With knot of two I ask of you
With knot of three, hear my plea
With knot of four I banish poor
With knot of five I am alive
With knot of six the spell is fixed
With knot of seven, money falls from Heaven
With knot of eight my financial life is great
With knot of nine I have enough money for me and mine

Now place the knotted cord inside your pillowcase for 9 days.

On the 10th day, remove the cord and dispose of it either by burying it near a stream of running water or burning it with the flame of a white candle.

Powerful Moon Money Spell

<u>You will need</u>:

New moon
Handful of change
Salt
White candle

<u>Instructions</u>:

Go outside where you have both a flat surface and a good view of the new moon.

Sprinkle the salt in a circle around you.

Place all the coins on the ground inside the circle.

Light your candle and hold it in your left hand. Say the following:

My luck will grow with this I know
That it is fate, for my wealth to be great

Repeat this 9 times, and blow out the candle.

Leave your circle of coins on the ground for 3 days.

On the 3rd day, collect the coins and carry them with you for another 9 days and money should follow them.

Spell For a Specific Amount of Money

You will need:

Green candle
Dime
Needle

Instructions:

Carve the specific amount of money you need into the side of the candle near the top.

Place the candle on your altar and the dime directly in front of the candle, touching it. Light the candle and say the following:

This mission of mine has taken time
Now I will the money come to me upon this dime

The candle should remain lit for at least 10 minutes. During this time, focus on the amount of money you need and your exact reason for needing it.

Each day burn the candle for another 10 minutes while focusing on the amount of money you need until the candle is gone.

Take the remaining wax and the dime and put them in any standing water or bury them at least a foot under ground. Within 30 days the specific amount of money should come to you.

Full Moon Money Chant

This can be done at any time. It is okay to say the words only in your mind if necessary, but better to speak them out loud if you are alone or feel comfortable doing so in company.

While looking up at a full moon, say the following:

Money money money is for me
Money money money come to me
Money money money is for me
I will tell nobody

Money Chant for Any Time

At any time, repeat the following words silently or out loud.

O Goddess, Inspire me
I call upon the money stream
Bring to me cash in reams
That I may have the riches I desire

Herbal Money Bath

Do not attempt this powerful money bath if you have sensitive skin or any skin condition.

You will need:

Ginger root
Cinnamon stick
Fresh basil
Bathtub

Instructions:

Run your bath however you normally would.

Add the herbs to the water, in any order. While adding your herbs, focus your mind on wealth.

Get in the water, and submerge yourself quickly. Do not stay under the water for more than a few seconds, and make sure your eyes are closed the entire time.

When you come back up, exit the bathtub. This powerful concoction of herbs may burn.

Simple Candle Spell to Bring Money II

You will need:

2 black candles
Needle
Sunday

Instructions:

Carve your name, the word "money" and any power words or symbols that are significant to you in both candles.

On any Sunday, light both candles and hold one in each hand. Say the following:

With these candles black
Money I will no longer lack
Bring to me cash
As quick as a flash

Meditate for a minute, longer if you feel it is necessary, while holding these candles. When you are done, snuff them out.

You can repeat this on any night afterwards, as long as the spell began on a Sunday, until you either received the money you needed or the candles burned down.

Rice Spell to Attract Money

You will need:

Handful of rice
White candle
Waxing moon
Altar

Instructions:

Scatter the rice on your altar and place the candle in the center of it.

Light the candle and then say the following 3 times:

I will see my money grow and grow

Allow the candle to burn at least 10 minutes, and then snuff it out.

If your candle is not finished the first night, relight it as many nights as it takes to finish for at least 10 minutes a night.

When the candle is done, carry the rice with you however you normally carry change, in a pocket or coin purse, for 7 days or until money comes to you, then sprinkle it outside around your home.

Spell for Money to Pay Bills

You will need:

Oil burner
Cedar oil
Gold candle

Instructions:

Begin by lighting your oil burner and candle. Meditate for a few moments and when you feel ready say the following:

O Goddess
Grant me money though not for greed
But just enough to fulfill my needs
Grant this wish and I will remember
To give as I have received

When the candle has burned down completely, you can extinguish the oil burner.

Spell for a Powerful Rock to Attract Money

You will need:

Any rock you found personally
Green paint or permanent market
Gold candle
Waxing moon
Darkness

Instructions:

Assemble everything together before you turn out the lights.

Light your candle and by the light of the flame paint or draw money symbols such as a dollar sign, any other currency sign, or any symbol which you relate to money on the top of the rock.

On one side of the rock write your name.

The candle should remain lit for at least 3 minutes after you have finished drawing on the rock, and then snuffed out.

Place your rock on a window (or outside if you must) where it can receive the light of the moon.

Leave the rock there for a complete cycle (28 days) to finish the spell. When the cycle is over, the rock can be buried on your property.

Mojo Bag to Draw Money to Pay Bills

You will need:

Green candle
Green ribbon or thread
Green cloth
Cinnamon oil
Dollar bill
5 pumpkin seeds
3 cinnamon sticks
Friday
Waxing moon

Instructions:

Carve your name and the words money, wealth, prosperity, or any other power words you wish into the candle.

Anoint the candle with cinnamon oil.

Light your candle and say the following:

Pumpkin seeds will do the deed
And cinnamon sticks will the trick
The money I need will come to me quick
So I will it, so mote it be

While chanting, place the dollar bill, pumpkin seeds, and cinnamon sticks on the cloth.

Fold the cloth over them 3 times and tie it together with the ribbon.

The candle should burn for at least 9 minutes, and then should be snuffed out.

Keep the mojo bag near the place where you normally pay your bills until you have received the money you need.

Candle Spell to Attract Wealth and Repel Poverty

You will need:

Green candle
Black candle
Needle

Instructions:

Carve the black candle with whatever you want to lose. Debt, high bills, anything that is affecting your finances negatively. You may use words or symbols.

Carve the green candle with your name and words or symbols relating to money. You can carve a specific need into the candle such as "microwave" or "cell phone" but it isn't necessary.

Place the black candle on the left side of the green one.

Light the black candle first, and meditate on it for a few moments while visualizing negativity flowing out and away from you.

Then light the green candle and meditate on it for a few moments while visualizing money flowing towards you, your needs being met, and general fulfillment.

Allow the candles to burn for up to an hour. If the candles aren't finished the first time, repeat nightly until they are burned down.

Candle Spell for Malachite and Power Coin

You will need:

Green candle
Oil of your choice
Malachite
Shiny penny

Instructions:

Carve your name into the candle and the word money or any other word you use for money.

Anoint the candle.

Place the candle in front of you and the malachite and penny in front of the candle.

Position the malachite to be touching the very base of the candle, so that wax will fall on it. The penny can be an inch away. Say the following:

Air, water, fire, and earth
Allow money to flow from the sky
See this penny, now multiply!

Allow the candle to burn completely and the wax to dry.

Take the wax and malachite (they should be melded together) and bury them on your property.

Carry the power penny with you in your pocket or purse daily.

Spell to be Repaid Money You Loaned

You will need:

Piece of paper
Gold candle
Green pen
Red pen
Needle
Candle holder
Saturday

Instructions:

Carve the words "repay my money (Name)" into the candle.

Take your red pen and write the borrower's full name 9 times on the piece of paper. Then turn the paper and cross over his name, writing the words 'repay my money' with your green pen 9 times.

Fold the paper into quarters.

Now light the candle and say the following:

Spirits of the Earth, hear me speak
(Full Name) shall be compelled to
Feel the burn of (his or her) conscience and
The sadness of (his or her) remorse
As (he or she) recalls the money owed to me
Repay my money to me (Full Name)

Now singe the edges of your folded paper, snuff your candle, and place the paper underneath the candle holder.

Repeat these steps every night, beginning on a Saturday, for 7 days. Each day, you should make every effort to reach out to the person who owes you money, and each night you should repeat the spell as directed above.

On the 7th night, as you say "Repay my money to me (Full Name)" burn up the paper completely.

New Moon Money Spell

You will need:

Silver coin
Cauldron
Water
New moon

Instructions:

On the night of the new moon, fill your cauldron halfway and go outside where there is a clear view of the moon.

In the moonlight, place your cauldron on the ground.

Put the silver coin in the cauldron and say the following:

Lovely Lady of the Moon
Bring me your wealth soon
Fill my hands with silver and gold
All that you give me, my purse will hold

While you are saying this, make a gathering motion with your hands as if you are gathering moonlight and placing it in your cauldron with the coin.

Repeat as many times as you feel necessary.

The cauldron and its contents should be left outside overnight to absorb the power of the moonlight.

In the morning the water can be poured out into the ground, and the coin should not be spent for at least 3 days.

Spell for a Specific Amount of Money II

You will need:

3 bay leaves
Piece of paper
Green pen
New moon

Instructions:

On the paper, write out exactly how much money you need and the reason.

Place the bay leaves on the paper and fold it in thirds.

Visualize your needs being met and everything working out okay.

Fold the paper and leaves in thirds again. Visualize again.

The paper should be stored in a dark, safe area until you receive the money that is needed.

Once the money is received, burn the paper and leaves.

Powerful Money Magnet Spell

You will need:

Small plain magnet
Gold candle

Instructions:

Carve power words for money or symbols for money into the candle.

Carve your name into the candle.

Light the candle and allow a small amount of wax to accumulate.

Press your right index finger into the wax, and then into the side of the candle. This will put your fingerprint on the candle and bind it and the spell to you.

With the candle now sitting in front of you, hold the magnet firmly in your hand. Say the following:

Goddess, Bless me
And grant me prosperity
I will receive
What I need
This will harm none
Let it be done!

Now carry the magnet with you in your purse or pocket until your monetary needs are met.

Annual Money Spell

<u>You will need</u>:

Corn husk
Green ribbon or thread
Piece of paper
Pen

<u>Instructions</u>:

Write on the piece of paper "Bring both wealth and health to (your address)."

Bind together the corn husk and paper with the green ribbon. The paper should be inside the corn husk.

Now attach this above the entrance door to your home or business and it will bring luck and money your way for the entire year.

Monthly Money Spell

You will need:

1st Sunday of the month
Green or gold candle
Flat stone
Needle

Instructions:

If you are doing this for the first time be careful selecting the flat rock because if you plan on doing this monthly you will be using the same rock each time. Also, when you choose between a green or gold candle, keep in mind you may be repeating the spell and will need to stick with that color of candle to make the spell grow in strength each time you do it. So you can choose either green or gold based on your current candle supplies.

Go outside in darkness or at least in low light.

Carve the candle with your name and the amount of money you need for the following month.

Place the candle on the rock, light it, and meditate on the fact that you will have enough the entire month. Visualize having enough money.

When the candle is burned down, place the rock outside your door. It doesn't matter if the wax side is up or down, as long as you pass the rock each time you go in or out of the doorway.

The rock should stay there at least a month. At the beginning of the next month, you can choose to repeat the spell.

Money Talisman for Success in Your Business

You will need:

2 red candles
2 white candles
Cinnamon oil
7 nickels
2 cups of white rice
Tablespoon of powdered sugar
Basil
Baking pan
Cloth bag

Instructions:

Spread the uncooked white rice into your baking pan.

Add the powdered sugar on top of it, and then add the basil on top of the sugar.

Make a circle inside the pan with the 7 coins.

Anoint your candles in cinnamon oil and place them in the corners of the pan. The 2 red candles should be at the top corners and the white candles in the bottom corners.

Light the candles and meditate while they burn completely down.

While meditating, you should visualize your financial life and all the things you wish for it to be. If you want to have 30 regular clients, imagine the work you would be doing if you had them. (Note: do not imagine *finding* the clients, visualize that you already have them and the work you would be doing.)

If your business is constantly struggling to pay bills, visualize paying all the bills. Picture writing checks or making online payments and not only having enough money to do it, but having money left over after it's done. Visualize everything you can think of.

When the candles are burned down, gather the coins and some rice, powdered sugar, and basil and place all of this in the cloth bag, which should then be kept at your place of business.

Spell For Home Repair Money

You will need:

Brown cloth bag or large square of cloth
9 coins
Green candle
Cinnamon
Access to a tree
Needle

Instructions:

Carve the amount of money you need for repairs into the side of the candle near the top. Below that, carve the reason you need the money but keep it simple. Something like "refrigerator" or "basement" is fine if you have a broken refrigerator or flooded basement. You do not need to be very detailed.

Place the 9 coins in a circle with the candle in the middle.

Light the candle and say the following:

I do this deed
I am in need
My money will flow
And it will grow

While repeating the chant, sprinkle your cloth or bag with the cinnamon and gather the coins to put inside.

Tie a knot at the top.

Continue repeating the chant and secure the bundle in a tree.

Leave the bag in the tree over night.

The following night, remove the bag and bury it at the base of the tree.

Lay a Money Trail to Your Door

You will need:

Sandalwood
Cinnamon
Mortar & pestle

Instructions:

Grind together 4 parts sandalwood to 1 part cinnamon. It doesn't have to be a huge amount, but enough to fill the small bowl.

Leave your house through the front door and go the nearest walkway. This could be a sidewalk, parking lot, or the end of your driveway.

When you reach this point, walk back to your front door sprinkling the powder behind you as you go.

Increase Wealth of Household

You will need:

Small amount of green paint
Full moon

Instructions:

Be warned this spell has the power to increase the wealth of everyone in the household.

On an evening the full moon is clearly visible, go outside and under its light paint your index finger with green paint. Go to your doorway and above it place your green fingerprint while saying:

Those who pass beneath
Have their personal wealth increased

Your fingerprint can be in an inconspicuous place if you live in someone else's house or an apartment. It doesn't have to be obvious unless you want it to be.

Love Powder for the Home

You will need:

Mortar & pestle
Rosemary
Basil
Rice
Lavender

Instructions:

Grind all ingredients finely.

Sprinkle this love dust in corners or across carpets.

As you are sprinkling this around, visualize your home filled with love, kindness, and hope. This will produce a fresh, clean, loving smell for your home.

Spell to Attract Love in the Home

You will need:

Small bowl
Handful of sesame seeds
Cinnamon stick
Red string
Morning

Instructions:

On any morning where you have time and don't feel rushed, assemble your ingredients together.

Place the sesame seeds in a bowl.

Tie the string around the cinnamon stick and knot it 3 times.

Place the cinnamon stick in the bowl on top of the sesame seeds.

Keep the bowl by the door you use most often as an entrance.

It must not be sitting on the ground, but elevated at least a few inches. You can set it on a small table, a windowsill, or even on top of a stack of books, so long as it is not directly on the floor.

Each time you exit your house, pause by the door and stir the sesame seeds with your finger.

Luck Powder for the Home

You will need:

Handful bay leaves
Ground up dollar bill
Dried rose petals
Dried juniper berries
Handful of sage
Mortar & pestle

Instructions:

Grind all ingredients finely. This can either be stored in a bowl in the room or space that you wish to make luckier, or else sprinkled in corners and under furniture. Replace monthly if necessary.

For a Peaceful Home

You will need:

Fresh cut parsley
Small bowl

Instructions:

Fill the bowl with water.

Add the parsley and allow it soak for half an hour.

Carry the pan around your home sprinkling water throughout the house, while picturing a peaceful environment.

Banishing Powder for the Home

You will need:

Equal parts pepper: black, white, cayenne, paprika, etc.
Wasabi powder equal to one part of pepper
Mortar & pestle

Instructions:

Grind together all ingredients finely. Sprinkle conservatively in corners or across doorways throughout your home while visualizing all negativity leaving the home and being unable to return. The dust should be invisible to the naked eye. Be sure and keep children and small pets away from areas where the dust was sprinkled as this dust is very hot. Wash hands after sprinkling.

Ghost Protection Powder

You will need:

1 part dried rosemary
1 part sea salt
1 part garlic powder
Mortar & pestle

Instructions:

Grind together all ingredients finely. Sprinkle this ghost repelling dust wherever you feel necessary in your home. This ritual can be repeated monthly.

Spell to Protect Your Home From Negativity

You will need:

White candle

Instructions:

Light the candle and take it to every entry point in the house, both doors and windows. Allow 3 drops of wax to fall in each entry way. Say the following each time wax drips:

By the power of three by three this spell will protect me and my family

The candle should be allowed to burn completely down when you are done with the wax drippings.

Spell to Find a Lover

You will need:

2 red candles
Red ribbon (about 18 inches)
Handful of rose petals
Needle
Altar

Instructions:

Carve your name into one of the candles, along with descriptive words that apply to you most. Are you ambitious, glamorous, or smart? You can add as many words as you feel like, but *they must apply to you*. Do not exaggerate.

Take the other candle and carve into it qualities you need in a partner. This may be things like athlete, moderate, easygoing. Make sure they are things you know you want.

Place the candles about a foot apart on your altar. Tie the ends of the ribbon loosely around both candles. You should end up with the two candles surrounded by the circle of ribbon with a knot.

Put your rose petals around the candles inside the ribbon circle.

Light the candles, and for 5 minutes focus on what *you have to offer* a mate. Do not exaggerate. You may do this for longer than 5 minutes if you feel it's necessary. Snuff your candles when done, and leave them in their exact positions, ribbon, rose petals, and all.

The next day, untie the ribbon, move the candles about an inch closer together, retie the ribbon, light the candles and repeat your 5 minutes of focusing on what you have to offer.

Continue every evening, untying and retying the ribbon while the candles move closer and closer together.

Eventually they will touch.

Once the candles are together, and have burned down the rest of the way together, your spell is complete.

If your candles burnt down before they touched, the spell is a failure and you need to repeat it with taller candles and more concentration on realistic goals.

Powerful Attraction Amulet

You will need:

Small piece of rose quartz

Instructions:

Keep the rose quartz under your pillow. Each night when you go to sleep, and each morning when you wake up touch the rose quartz.

Spend a few minutes concentrating on the person you wish to attract. Then say:

All the love that I send out
Shall multiply by three
I will find you and you will love me with no doubt
So mote it be

Do this for 7 days. At the end of 7 days you will have finished the spell and have a power amulet of attraction. You can fasten the rose quartz to a necklace or bracelet, or wear it in a pouch around your neck. It can also be carried in a pocket or purse.

This spell can also be completed with a small piece of amber.

Amber will generally attract a relationship while rose quartz will attract a romantic relationship.

Spell to Attract a Specific Person

You will need:

Red candle
Rose oil
Apple
Altar

Instructions:

Anoint your candle with rose oil and place it on your altar to the right of the apple. Light the candle.

Spend a few minutes visualizing the specific person you would like to attract in your mind. Don't proceed until the picture is perfect. Say the following:

My love is true and by the burning flame
O Goddess I ask that (Full Name) feel the same
Scent of the rose, be carried far by fire
That your love for me will grow and so will your desire

Repeat this 3 times and snuff out the candle. Take the apple to a window that allows moonlight to enter. Leave the apple overnight so that it draws power from the moon.

In the morning consume the apple, saving the seeds. Plant each seed and care for it, as seedlings sprout, love in your life will sprout also.

Spell to Attract a Specific Man

You will need:

Red candle
Picture of him
Piece of paper
Red lipstick
New moon

Instructions:

Light the candle, and spend a few minutes focusing your will on him.

Once you feel very focused and clear, burn his picture in candle.

Apply lipstick and kiss the paper.

Fold it in quarters and burn in.

Sweep up the ashes of the picture and paper and go outside to face the moon.

With your hand above your head, let go of the ashes while saying:

I am in love with you and my love is true
By the power of this spell, you will love me too

Spell for an Amber Amulet to Attract a Lover

You will need:

Small chunk of amber
Sprig of rosemary
Sprig of lavender
Rose petals
Jar of honey (not filled to the top)
Jar of water
Piece of paper
Red pen
Black pen
Red candle
Moonlight (waxing moon works best)

Instructions:

On the left half of the piece of paper, write out all of the qualities you have to offer a man or a woman in black ink. Be specific and don't exaggerate.

On the right side of the paper, write in red all of the qualities you seek in a partner.

Fold the paper in quarters.

Seal the paper closed with dripping wax from the red candle.

Open your jar of honey.

Sink the paper into the honey saying *"I cast this spell with the best intent"*
Add the rose petals saying *"through these petals I will soon see"*
Add the rosemary saying *"the way to the one for whom I am meant"*
Add the lavender saying *"so mote it be"*
Last add the amber to the honey and seal the jar.

Go outside under the light of moon, and bury the jar of honey.

Place the jar of water on top of the ground to mark the spot where the honey rests, and to absorb the moonlight.

On the 9th night dig up your jar, remove the amber and wash it in the water that has been bathed in moonlight. You now have a powerful amulet of attraction. Wear this around your neck or wrist.

To Call Your Soul Mate

You will need:

White candle
Red candle
Handful of rose petals
Vanilla incense
Sandalwood oil
Friday
Visible Moon
Bowl

Instructions:

Begin by lighting the vanilla incense.

Place your rose petals in the bowl.

Anoint the red candle with sandalwood oil.

Hold the red candle (unlit) and visualize your soul mate.

Once you are relaxed and have a clear picture in your mind, you may proceed.

Light the red candle and place it near the bowl and incense.

Now take the unlit white candle and make a circular motion around the red candle, making smaller and smaller circles as you go around.

Once the candles have made contact light the white candle with the flame of the red candle and place the white candle on the right side of the red one. You should be focused and visualizing the entire time.

When the candles have burned down fully (you may leave while they finish) take the rose petals and sprinkle them under your bed. Allow them to remain over the weekend. On Monday, take a relaxing bath with the petals to finish the spell.

Spell to Find a New Lover II

You will need:

Red paper heart
Pink candle
Piece of paper
Red pen
Envelope
New moon

Instructions:

Light the candle.

Write on the piece of paper "I call a new lover tonight."

Place the paper and the red heart in the envelope.

Seal the envelope with wax, and place your thumbprint in the wax to bind yourself fully to the spell.

The envelope should be stored in a safe place. When the new love comes into your life, burn the envelope and its contents as a thank you.

Simple Spell to Find a Mate

<u>You will need:</u>

White candle
Candle of your choice
Ground rosemary
Red or pink altar cloth

<u>Instructions</u>:

The white candle represents your mate and the other candle represents yourself. Place the candles on the altar about a foot apart, the white candle on the left side.

Dust the rosemary around both candle holders.

When your mind is calm and ready, light the candle representing yourself.

Focus on all the qualities you have to offer a mate, and speak them out loud in a firm voice.

Next light the white candle. Project all of your qualities into the white candle.

Now, speak out loud all the qualities you are looking for in a mate.

When you are done, snuff the candles. Leave everything in its place overnight.

The second night, move the candles closer together, though still in the circle, to about 6 inches apart. Repeat the process of stating out loud what you have to offer, and what you are looking for. When you are finished, snuff the candles.

On the third night, move the candles where they are touching each other. Go over the same process. This time, allow the two candles to burn down fully while touching each other and your spell is complete.

For a Powerful Silver Ring to Attract a Soul Mate (for Women)

You will need:

Silver ring
White wine
White cloth
Full moon
Black candle

Instructions:

In the light of the moon, wrap the silver ring inside the white cloth and bury it. While pouring white wine over the ground where the ring is buried, say the following:

O Moonlight, by your shine
I bury a silver ring
So that you can grant me what is mine
Send me a lover, who will be my king

Leave the ring where it is for a full 28 days. Then you may return to the spot where the ring is buried.

Burn the black candle over the ground where the ring is buried to remove negativity from the area. Dig up the ring.

Place the black candle wax in the hole in place of the ring, and wear the ring on your finger to attract a soul mate.

Candle Spell to Change Dating Luck

You will need:

Silver candle if you are female, gold candle if you are a male
Black candle
Orange candle
Magenta candle

Instructions:

Carve the black candle with anything in your life you want to lose.

Carve the silver or gold candle with your name.

Arrange the candles in a circle with the silver or gold candle at 12:00, the black candle at 3:00, the orange candle at 6:00 and the magenta candle at 9:00.

As you light the silver or gold candle say:
This candle represents me

As you light the black candle say:
This candle represents negativity
It will burn up
Leaving me with only good luck

As you light the orange candle say:
This candle represents dynamic change
Which I welcome entirely

As you light the magenta candle say:
And this candle represents speed
So that change will quickly fill my needs

Allow the candles to burn all the way down and the spell is finished.

Spell to be Attractive to the One You Love

You will need:

Red ribbon 1 foot long
Live rose
2 petals from the rose
3 red candles
Sandalwood oil
Needle

Instructions:

Carve your name into a candle, your love's name into another, and love words or symbols into the last candle. Love words could be anything that feels right to you such as: love, life, attraction, lover, passion, family, hope, or joy. These are simply examples. Carve at least 3 powerful love words or symbols.

Anoint the candles in sandalwood oil.

Form a circle with the piece of red ribbon. Place the petals and the candles inside the circle. Light the candles and say the following:

I live in great fear
That you will not be my dear

With this spell I cast
I ask that you notice me at last

I offer you my best
And will wait to see if you can handle the rest

Allow the candles to burn all the way down. Save the 2 rose petals to add to your bath. After bathing yourself, give the rose to the one you love to finish the spell.

To Break a Love Curse

<u>You will need</u>:

2 red candles
9 pine needles
Bowl or cauldron
3 red roses
Thursday

<u>Instructions</u>:

On any Thursday evening, light both red candles.

Burn the 9 pine needles in the bowl or cauldron.

Once they are burned, offer up the 3 red roses to Aphrodite. The roses represent the Maiden, the Mother, and the Crone. Once they have been offered, you can appeal directly to Aphrodite.

If you have done something wrong in respect to Love, this is the time to confess it. This could be anything: being unreasonably annoyed or irritable towards a lover, cheating on a lover, or physically or mentally abusing them. Everything that occurs to you, you should confess honestly, without making excuses.

Once you have confessed, offer up any commitments you can. If you have lied to a lover, make a promise to Aphrodite that you will not lie to your next lover. You can promise anything you like, but it must be something you are able to fulfill. You could promise to shower a lover with your love and kisses and commitments, or promise to bring forth children and care for them as best you can.

When you are done making your commitments, kindly ask that the curse and bad luck working against you be removed and replaced with neutrality. Be careful that you never break your word to Aphrodite.

Monthly Love Spell

<u>You will need</u>:

Friday evening
Waxing moon
2 red candles
Needle
Bowl or cauldron

<u>Instructions</u>:

Melt the red candles into your cauldron or bowl and allow the wax to cool enough to touch but not become totally hard.

When the wax is cool enough, take it and form it into the shape of a heart.

Once it is in the form of a heart, allow it to cool totally.

Take the needle and carve your initials and your lover's initials into the wax.

Place the wax heart near your bed and keep it there.

This spell can be repeated monthly and will keep your relationship strong and passionate.

Spell to Bury Troubles With a Lover

You will need:

Black candle
Small cloth bag
Apple seeds from an apple you ate yourself
2 small pieces of paper
Red pen

Instructions:

Carve the black candle with anything you want to lose in the relationship. This can be things like arguments, jealousy, whatever is troubling you.

Light the candle and as it burns down visualize having the perfect relationship with your lover. Don't proceed until you have imagined the perfect relationship.

You have released the negativity plaguing the relationship.

Now, write your full name on one paper and cross it with any love words or special words between you and your lover.

Write their full name on the other piece of paper and again cross it with love words.

Place the papers with the written sides together in the bag along with the apple seeds.

This should be buried outside and the rift will be healed.

Lover's Bottle to Strengthen a Relationship

You will need:

Glass bottle with corked top
Rosewater
Petals of a flower you received from your lover
Sprig of lavender
Sprig of rosemary
Cinnamon stick
Red candle

Instructions:

Light the candle.

Assemble the ingredients together and spend a few minutes with your eyes closed to relax before starting. Visualize yourself and your lover as being a strong, confident couple.

When you are ready, fill the bottle with rosewater almost to the top.

Add the petals, lavender, rosemary, and cinnamon stick. If the bottle is not filled after these things have been added, fill to the top with rosewater.

Cork the bottle and seal the cork with wax.

Keep the bottle sealed up and in a location where you see it frequently. It's okay to give it to your lover if you wish. Special care should be taken to keep the bottle intact.

Spell to Sweeten an Existing Relationship

You will need:

A clear glass of water, covered
Green candle
Black candle
Bowl that will easily hold your candle
Piece of paper
Green pen
Full moon
Needle

Instructions:

Leave the clear glass of water outside, exposed to moonlight, for at least 1 hour. After 1 hour or more, bring the water indoors.

Carve your lover's name into the green candle.

Write your name on the paper.

Stand the candle in the bowl and light it.

Now spend a few minutes, as long as it takes, visualizing yourself, your lover, perfect harmony and happiness.

When you have a clear picture in your mind of happiness, shred the paper with your name on it and place it in the bowl surrounding the candle.

Add half of the water to the bowl.

Consume the remaining water.

Allow the candle to burn down.

When the green candle has burned, light the black candle in its place (still over the water and paper mixture) and allow it to burn completely to remove any negativity.

Spell to Make a Current Relationship Stronger

You will need:

3 red candles
2 pink candles
Photo of yourself
Photo of your lover
Red ribbon

Instructions:

Place the candles in the shape of a pentacle, so that if lines were drawn between them they would form a star. The red candles should be placed at the top and bottom points of the star and the pink candles at the left and right points.

Place the photos in the center of the candles. Say the following:

I call on the power of fire
to keep me with the one that I desire

Our souls shall join together
so that we may depend on each other forever

Though sometimes we may be wrong
our relationship shall remain forever strong

Let us not be broken apart by lies
and stay together until one of us dies

Though at times it may be scary
we are bound together until one of us is buried

Using the candle from the top point of the pentacle, allow wax to drip on the front of your lover's photo, and make an imprint there with your finger.

Place your photo on top of your lovers, so that they face each other and create a wax seal. Bind them together with ribbon.

The photos should not be allowed to become unbound, and should be always kept in a dark and safe place.

Spell to Light a Fire in Your Love Life

You will need:

Cauldron
Paper
Red pen
Moonlight

Instructions:

Light a fire in your cauldron. Write your name and your lover's name on the paper and surround them with a heart shape. Fold the paper in quarters and place it in the fire. Then say the following:

With this Fire
I ignite my desire

It is you I need
Now come to me please
In my eyes you see
All there is to me
My love for you shines
And you will always be mine

By the power of this flame
I lay down my claim

With your eyes now closed, meditate on your relationship and imagine it truly filled with happiness and passion. Allow the flames to burn out naturally to finish the spell.

Spell to Bring Back a Lover

You will need:

2 white candles
Photo of lover
Photo of yourself
Red cloth
Chamomile teabag
Evening

Instructions:

Any evening, light the 2 white candles.

Close your eyes and visualize yourself and your former lover in a peaceful and relaxing environment. When you are ready, open your eyes and say the following:

By the light of the flame
I call out your name
With the will of my fire
You think of me with great desire

Now place the 2 photos facing each other and the chamomile teabag in the red cloth and tie it all together. Keep this packet in a safe place. To strengthen this spell, you can burn a red candle each evening while meditating on your lover.

To Heal a Relationship

You will need:

Cauldron
Water
New moon

Instructions:

On the night of the new moon, fill your cauldron halfway and go outside where there is a clear view of the moon. In the moonlight, place your cauldron on the ground. Say the following:

Lovely Lady of the Moon
I ask your help, I need it soon

Send love down to me
So that I may see

Where I have gone wrong
And how to be strong

While you are saying this, make a gathering motion with your hands as if you are gathering moonlight and placing it in your cauldron. Repeat as many times as you feel necessary.

Then, visualize your relationship being healed.

When you are ready, return to the indoors and consume the water.

Annual Love Spell: Bonding Jar

You will need:

Blue or green pen
Red pen
White paper
Jar of honey

Instructions:

This spell will keep you and your lover bound tightly together and in a sweet relationship. This can be done only once per year.

Take the paper and write both of your full names on it in either blue or green pen.

Using the red pen, cross your names with love words that apply to your relationship. These could be any meaningful words to you, such as: baby, lust, lover, soul mate, heart, life, happiness, or whatever you feel like.

Surround the names and crossed over words with a heart shape, then another heart around that.

Fold the paper into quarters and place it in the honey jar.

If you like, you can write the date on the outside of the jar, you will need a permanent marker if you choose to do this. Keep the jar in a safe place for at least one year. At the end of the year, if you wish to make another jar you must first throw this jar into deep water. Only at the point can you create a second bonding jar.

Be Unforgettable

You will need:

Small clear bottle filled with water
Sprig of rosemary
Red dye
Salt

Instructions:

Place the bottle in front of you and circle it with salt.

Close your eyes and visualize yourself and all of your best qualities.

When you feel ready, put 2 drops of red dye into the water followed by the sprig of rosemary.

Say the following:

With these words I plead
For you to think of me
Always I remain in your heart
As you have been in mine from the start

And if you should ever start to forget me
I will appear before your eyes and you will see
There was never another for you but me
As I will it, so mote it be

Now take this bottle and bury it near or on the property where your lover resides. So long as it remains buried there undisturbed you will be unforgettable in their mind.

Spell to Keep a Husband Loyal

:

Apple
Lock of your hair tied with a white ribbon
Lock of your husband's hair tied with a pink ribbon
3 white candles
Handful of rose petals
Cinnamon oil
White cord 12 inches long
Needle

Instructions:

Anoint the candles with cinnamon oil.

Carve your name into one, your husband's name into the next. The third candle should be carved with love words.

Halve the apple and core out the halves.

Place the lock of your husband's hair and the rose petals in one half, and your hair into the other half.

Tie the apple back together with everything securely inside using the white cord.

Pass the apple through the flames of the 3 white candles while visualizing yourself, your husband, and your happy marriage.

When you are done visualizing, bury the apple outside your bedroom window.

Spell to Increase Chance of Conception

You will need:

Man and woman who wish to conceive
Baby blanket, pink for girls and blue for boys
Piece of paper
Black pen
Silver cup
Spoon
3 red candles
Handful of rose petals
Pitcher of holy water

Instructions:

Both people need to know and understand how the spell is going to work before beginning, as it is to be done in silence.

In a private area, where it is just the two of you, spread out the blanket. The couple should be sitting on opposite sides of the blanket, facing each other.

On the paper, either person should draw a pentacle and then write their name on it. Then the second person should add their name to the pentacle.

Place the pentacle in the center of the blanket and place the silver cup on top of it. Now fill the cup with holy water.

To the right side of the couple, but not on the blanket, light the 3 red candles.

The female who wishes to become pregnant should crush the rose petals with her hands, and when they are thoroughly crushed add them to the holy water.

The male should stir the roses together with the holy water.

After the water and roses are mixed, the female should lie along her side of the blanket and remove her shirt. The male should take the cup and move near her. Together, the couple says out loud:

Baby, baby, baby, come to us
We will give you a good life
And you can take that in trust

Then the female says out loud:

O Goddess, hear my plea
Send a baby to me!
So I will it
So mote it be!

The male should take the holy water with rose petals and gently massage it on the naked flesh of the female, paying particular interest to her stomach and breasts.

Now the couple should make an attempt to conceive on their blanket, while the candles remain lit behind them.

Spell for a Female Who Wishes to Become Pregnant

You will need:

2 sticks of sandalwood incense
White candle
Fresh fig
Fresh egg
Clear bowl
Black marker
Dagger or boline
Trowel or spade
Instructions:

Light the candle and incense.

Directly in front of you and starting on your left, place the egg, then the bowl (center), then the fig (right).

Using your black marker, take the egg and draw on it anything that symbolizes a baby or becoming pregnant, or write out words such as "baby" or "conceive" on the egg. Hold the egg in your hands and visualize your child.

Carefully crack the egg into the bowl, placing the shell back on your left.

Cut into the fig using your dagger or boline, scraping the seeds into the bowl with your trowel or spade.

The fig remnants should be placed inside the eggshell.

Spend a few minutes meditating on becoming pregnant and having a child. When you feel ready, take the eggshell, fig remnants, and bowl outside to a safe place.

They should be buried in complete silence.

The candle and incense should be allowed to burn down totally to finish the spell.

Spell for a Couple to Bring a Baby

You will need:

Red wine
Glass or cup
Knife
Red candle
White candle
Man and woman who wish to conceive

Instructions:

The female should fill the glass with wine, and place the white candle to the left of the red one. The male should also stand on her left.

She should then prick her finger and add a drop of blood to the wine. Following that, she should prick the male's finger and add a drop of his blood as well.

Together the couple should say:

With love we offer our blood
our intent is to give life to another

The male should then light the white candle and say:

I am to be the father
and light this candle to give balance
to me and the mother

The female should light the red candle and say:

I am to be the mother
and light this candle to give happiness
to me and the father

The female hands the goblet to the male and says:

With this goblet we call forth our child

The male should drink half the wine and hand the glass back to the female and say:

With this goblet we call forth our child

The female drinks the remaining wine and then both say together:

So we will it, so mote it be.

Rainwater Conception Spell for Females

<u>You will need</u>:

Rainwater collected from the last rainfall
Full moon

<u>Instructions</u>:

Store the rainwater in a tightly sealed container in the refrigerator until the full moon.

On the night of the full moon, place the rainwater outside where it is exposed to moonlight overnight.

The following day, bring the rainwater back inside.

Stand naked in your bathtub with the container of water and visualize yourself holding your child.

Once you have a clear visual, pour the water over your head.

Ritual to Increase Chance of Conception

You will need:

Sandalwood incense
Gold candle
Silver candle

Instructions:

Each time before you make an attempt at conception perform this ritual.

The gold candle should be placed on the left.

Light the gold candle, the silver candle, and the incense. Both people should close their eyes and visualize having a child.

When both people are ready, continue on with your attempt.

For Good Luck in a Court Case

You will need:

Many pieces of paper
Black pen
Orange candle
Scissors
Cauldron or fire safe dish

Instructions:

In a quiet space, sit quietly and light the candle. Focus on calming down if you are not already calm. Do not proceed until you are in a calm state of mind.

Visualize each person involved in the legal case. When you see each person, see their point of view as well. Do not proceed to the next individual until you have fully visualized the current person and thought over their viewpoints as best as you can.

Next visualize each possible outcome, no matter how unlikely. Do not proceed until you have visualized every possible outcome. No matter what the outcome you are visualizing, remain in a calm state of mind.

Now, write down each outcome on a separate piece of paper as you have visualized it, remaining calm and clear the entire time.

When you have committed each scenario to paper, review all of them. Remember to remain calm and focused.

Choose the outcome you would like to see. Hold the paper in front of you and silently ask that this outcome be granted.

Fold the paper in quarters and place it under the candle.

Take the remaining outcomes and cut them into tiny pieces, which you should then burn in your cauldron.

Carry the folded paper with your desired outcome with you when you attend court.

Basic Wishing Spell

You will need:

3 white candles
2 candles with colors that relate to your wish
Black pen
Piece of paper
Bowl of water

Instructions:

The candles should be positioned in the shape of a pentacle, with the white candles forming the top and bottom points and the colored candles forming the left and right points.

Light the candles starting at the top point and moving clockwise.

Write your wish on the paper.

Focusing on the candles and holding the paper with your wish, visualize your wish coming true. Say the following:

On this paper my wish is told
And from no aspect of my heart should it withhold
I ask for fast fruition
So that my life may match my vision

Light the paper with your wish on fire, and douse it in the bowl of water.

The candles should be snuffed in the same order they were lit, and the bowl of water with ashes of the wish should be poured down a drain under a running tap.

Increasing the Luck of Any Object

You will need:

5 orange candles
Bowl of moon water
Your object

Instructions:

To create your moon water, leave a sealed container of water outside to absorb the light of the full moon. The water must remain outside over night.

The orange candles should be arranged to form the shape of a pentacle.

The bowl of moon water should be placed in the center of it, and your object in the water. Light the candles and say the following:

By the power of sun
Infuse this (name of object) with good luck

By the power of the moon
Infuse this (name of object) with magic

This will harm none
So it be done!

The object should be left overnight and will be ready the following morning.

Fast Luck Anklet

You will need:

Red thread 1 foot in length

Instructions:

Tie a knot in the thread while saying:
With knot of one I ask for luck

Tie a knot in the thread while saying:
With knot of two bring me wealth

Tie a knot in the thread while saying:
With knot of three I draw love

Tie a knot in the thread while saying:
With knot of four I keep my health

Keep the knotted cord in a mojo bag or tie it around your ankle. If the thread falls off your ankle, repeat instructions and replace it if necessary.

To Create Powerful Oil for Candle Dressing

You will need:

Peppermint or wintergreen oil
Vanilla oil
Cinnamon oil
Almond oil
Silver glitter

Instructions:

Combine one ounce almond oil with 10 drops of peppermint *or* wintergreen oil, 10 drops of vanilla oil, 10 drops of cinnamon oil, and a pinch of silver glitter. This powerful oil can be used to dress candles you want to use in money, luck, or power spells.

Spell to Increase a Specific Skill

You will need:

3 fresh oak leaves
3 yellow candles

Instructions:

Arrange the yellow candles to form a triangle and place the oak leaves in the center of it.

Light the candles starting at the top point of the triangle and moving clockwise. Say the following:

Spirit of (Skill) I call upon you
Gift me with your ability
I will use it with virtue and honor

Gift me with (Skill) Spirit
So I ask it
So mote it be

Snuff the candles and roll up the oak leaves, which should then be buried near your home.

Spell to Make Powerful Tea

You will need:

Cup of tea you made

Instructions:

Move your hand clockwise 3 times over the tea while saying:

I am the tool
You are the fire
In this cup
Is all I desire

Consume the tea. Your powers will receive a temporary boost after drinking this. It is best drunk before any spell casting to increase your power and influence over the spell.

Spell to Ward Off Stress

You will need:

Small cloth bag you made yourself
Handful of dirt from your yard
Dried flowers you picked yourself

Instructions:

Sewing this bag yourself will make your spell more powerful. To add additional strength, sew your initials on the bag in a bright color you feel represents you. The bag can be very simply made, not much talent is required. The important thing is to create it yourself.

When your bag is ready add the dirt and dried flowers and tie it closed.

This talisman can be carried with you, stored at work, or kept at home. During stressful moments reach out and touch the bag, taking a few calming breaths.

Spell to Create Happiness Amulet

<u>You will need</u>:

Bowl
Water
Sea salt
Amulet of your choice
Full moon

<u>Instructions</u>:

Place the amulet in the bowl and fill it with water.

Take the bowl outside during daylight where it will be exposed to the sun.

When the full moon rises go to your bowl and add sea salt to the water.

Stand before the moonlight and bowl and visualize complete happiness and peace in your life. Leave everything as it is over night.

When the bowl has been outside for full day, you can remove and dry off the amulet. You now have a powerful happiness charm. The water can be poured outdoors and watering a plant with it is fine.

Banish Black Magic

<u>You will need</u>:

White candle
Any oil you choose
Image of Saint Michael
Piece of quartz
Christian Bible or copy of the 91st Psalm

<u>Instructions</u>:

It is fine to print any image of Saint Michael you find online. You don't have to go buy anything.

Prop the image of Saint Michael anywhere.

Recite the 91st Psalm and light the candle. Say the following:

Saint Michael the Archangel
Defend me in Battle
Be my protection against wickedness and evil
Banish negativity or any evil spirit from my presence

The candle should be snuffed out. If you still feel there is negative energy around you, this spell may be repeated daily.

Space Cleansing Spell

You will need:

White candle
Sage incense
Bowl of water with salt
Wooden spoon

Instructions:

Place the candle to the left of the incense and light both.

Place the bowl in front of the candle and incense.

Stir the salt water with your wooden spoon. Close your eyes and visualize a bright white light rising from the bowl, expanding as it rises, filling the room you are in and surrounding you with a positive energy. Say the following:

Angels of the light
Remove all spirits who don't belong here

The chant can be repeated as many times as you feel necessary. Continue to chant with your eyes closed while visualizing the white light protecting you.

The candle and incense should be allowed to burn down.

Spell to Break a Hex Against You

You will need:

Small apple twig
Strand of your hair

Instructions:

While wrapping your hair around the apple twig, say the following:

Whoever it is that vexes me
Could vex themselves by the power of three
As I wish to harm none
I will bind their power
To a neutral tree

The twig with your hair around it should be placed in the nearest tree to where you sleep.

Spell to Banish a Bad Habit

You will need:

White candle
Black candle
Green candle
Waning moon

Instructions:

Begin by setting the candles in front of you from left to right: white, black, and green.

Meditate on the habit you wish to get rid of. Most habits are our own faults, though so often we are able to easily blame another, or blame no one, for these habits. Try and discover the reason you have this habit. What need does it satisfy in you? Do you really need this? Is there another way you could have this particular need satisfied, without this habit? Work through these issues silently and make a commitment to yourself to change.

Light the white candle. This represents you, the change you are making, the positive energy you will use to bring about this change and the strength to see it through. Meditate on this.

Light the black candle. The black candle represents negativity, the bad habit, and energy which can work against you while you break this habit. Visualize all negativity as well as the habit flowing away from you.

Light the green candle. This is your soul, and the change you have incurred in yourself. See yourself as though you are free of the habit.

Continue meditating while the candles burn down.

If you find yourself having difficulty breaking your habit during the next moon cycle, repeat this spell at the next waning moon.

Spell to Banish a Thing or Person From Your Life

You will need:

Cup of vinegar
Small piece of paper
Black pen
Bottle with seal

Instructions:

Write the name of the thing or person on the paper.

Fold the paper in half, making the fold go away from your body. Fold the paper a second time, again making the fold go away from your body.

Pour the cup of vinegar into the bottle and push the paper inside the bottle as well. If you have to cram it in and it ruins the folds, that's okay.

Shake the bottle to make sure the paper is entirely soaked in vinegar and say the following:

I banish thee for seven nights and seven days
You shall stay away!

The bottle should be buried somewhere on your property for 7 days.

On the 8th day, bring the bottle back inside and pour the vinegar down the toilet and flush it away.

Allow the paper to dry enough to burn. As soon as you are able, burn the paper and flush the ashes down the toilet as well, visualizing the thing or person leaving your life and never returning. Say the following:

For seven nights and seven days
You have stayed far away
You flee before me, I have gotten my way!

Spell to Avoid Danger

You will need:

9 dried apple seeds
Glass bottle
Water
Teaspoon of honey
Piece of paper
Any living vine 2 feet in length

Instructions:

Write what you want to avoid on the paper, roll it, and put it in the bottle.

Add the apple seeds and honey to the bottle, which should be filled halfway with water.

Add the cut end of the vine to the bottle so that it reaches the water.

Place the bottle in a place where it gets sunlight.

As long as the vine remains green you have protection. If you still feel the need to avoid your specific thing or situation and the vine dies, repeat the spell until the threat is over.

Protection Chant

This chant can be used at any time you feel the need for extra protection. You can repeat it silently to yourself or say it out loud.

Visualize a ring of white light surrounding your head. Visualize a second ring of white light surrounding your center. Visualize a third ring surrounding your ankles. Say silently or out loud:

Three times the rings go round
All evil shall stay on the ground
If any evil is around this place
It cannot enter my safety space
Three times three
So mote it be

Stones to Protect a Specific Area

You will need:

3 stones at least 2 inches wide
Cup of tea (your choice)
Red marker

Instructions:

Touch each stone to the tea, dry them, and set them aside.

Consume the tea.

Say the following:

I cast this stone
It is buried to protect my zone
And wherever this stone shall lie
No evil will be allowed to pass by
This is my safe place
And no evil is allowed in this space

Draw a pentacle on each of the three stones with your marker.

The stones should be buried so that they form a line behind which the space is now protected.

Spell to Defend Against Nightmares

You will need:

Dash of lemon juice
Dash of olive oil
Pinch of salt
Cauldron
2 small pieces of paper
Red candle
Black candle
Pen

Instructions:

Add the lemon juice, olive oil, and salt to your cauldron which should be placed directly in front of you.

Place red candle on the left and the black candle on the right and light them both.

On a piece of paper, draw out your biggest nightmare fear. Hold it in front of your face when you're done drawing and say "*Goodbye!*"

Burn this paper with the flame of the red candle and put the ashes in the cauldron.

On the other paper, write out your biggest nightmare fear. Hold it in front of your face when you're done writing and say "*Goodbye!*"

Burn this paper with the flame of the black candle and put the ashes in the cauldron.

When the papers are sufficiently burned, take the cauldron outside and dump the contents into dirt.

Spell to Cleanse a Specific Area

You will need:

White candle
Fireproof bowl or cauldron
Tablespoon garlic
Tablespoon peppermint
Tablespoon ground clove
Tablespoon dried thistle
3 dried oak leaves, crumbled

Instructions:

Put the garlic, peppermint, clove, thistle, and oak leaves into the cauldron.

Place the candle in the cauldron and light the herb mixture so it begins to smolder, and also the candle.

The cauldron or bowl should be placed in the center of the space you wish to cleanse. Say the following:

Mother of the Earth
Consecrate and cleanse this space
So that nothing but joy lingers here

Allow the candle to burn down and take it and the ashes and scatter them outside.

To Solve a Problem in a Dream

You will need:

Glass bottle
Rose petals
Yellow piece of paper
Black pen

Instructions:

Boil the rose petals and add the rose water to the glass bottle. This should be sealed and placed by your bed, at head level. If you don't have a nightstand, improvise in some way so that the bottle is raised up off the floor about the same as your head will be when you are sleeping.

Take the yellow paper and write out your problem. Be specific. Fold this in quarters and put it under the bottle of rose water.

Before you go to sleep, lie in bed and review your problem and possible solutions. Touch the rose water bottle and then sleep. When you wake up, the answer should become clear.

Spell to Increase Vivid Dreams

You will need:

4 white ribbons 1 foot in length each
4 pins unless your bed has posts

Instructions:

If your bed has posts, tie a ribbon on each post. If it doesn't have posts, pin a ribbon in each corner.

Each night before going to sleep, touch each ribbon and say:

Grant me powers which are hidden
Dreams come to me throughout the night
Grant me powers with each ribbon
To remember my dreams and remember them right

After 7 days, if you still need the ribbons, start again with fresh ones.

Dream Charm for Kids

You will need:

Small blue cloth bag
Blue or white ribbon
Small stone (preferable to have the child find it)
Silver glitter and stars
Dried rose petals
Small piece of quartz
Small piece of tiger's eye

Instructions:

Discuss with the child how wonderful good dreams are and their good dreams specifically. Tell the child that together, you are going to create a special dream charm to enhance good dreams and decrease bad dreams or nightmares.

Gather all the materials together and if possible, have the child add everything but the ribbon to the bag. If the child is too young to do this, you can do it for them explaining items as you go.

Have the child (if possible) tie the ribbon around the top of the bag and close it with three knots.

This should be kept under the child's pillow. Each night, have the child (if possible) touch it and say:

Bringer of bad dreams you cannot cause me fear
Bringer of good dreams you are always welcome here

Dream Charm for Vivid Dreams

You will need:

Small cloth bag of any color
Pinch of dried peppermint
Pinch of marigold
Pinch of lemon verbena
Pinch of lavender flowers
Cinnamon stick
Full moon

Instructions:

Outside under the light of the full moon, combine all ingredients in the cloth bag and close it.

This should be kept under your pillow, and rubbed over your 3rd eye each night before you fall asleep.

Spell to Increase Personal Energy

You will need:

As many white candles as it takes to form a circle around you sitting on the floor
Magenta candle
Frankincense oil

Instructions:

Anoint the candles with frankincense oil.

Form a circle around yourself with the white candles.

The magenta candle should be placed in the center.

Light all the candles.

Sit in the center and meditate. Think about yourself, your successes and failures and how you can personally improve. Envision the energy of the room swirling around you and then being absorbed by you. Continue meditating until the candles have burned down.

Spell to Energize an Object

You will need:

Bowl of water
Bowl of salt
White candle
Patchouli incense
Your object

Instructions:

Light the candle and incense.

Take your object and cover it with salt from the bowl. Visualize energy entering the object from your hand and the air around you. The salt will purify any negative energy. Then say:

With salt and smoke I consecrate this tool which will serve me well

Shake the salt off the object back into the bowl.

Pass the object through the smoke from the incense.

Sprinkle the object with water.

Pass it through the flame.

Your object is energized.

Spell to Draw Energy From the Moon

You will need:

Vegetable or olive oil
5 candles in a color representing you
Cup of any tea
Full moon

Instructions:

During a full moon, use your finger to draw a pentacle on a flat surface in oil.

Place the candles in the points of the pentacle and light them.

Place the tea in the center. Say the following:

Lovely Lady of the Moon
Please grant me a boon

Imbue me with your powers
That will allow my energy to flower

I ask that your energy be sent
Which I will only use with good intent

Allow the candles to burn down and consume the tea.

Chant to Increase Creative Energy

Chant the following at any time, either out loud or silently:

Goddess Brigid, giver of the gift of creativity
Bestow your gifts upon me
So that your energy will flow from me

Chant to Overcome Low Energy

This is only to be used when you are actually feeling drained or experiencing low energy. This chant will raise your energy back to what it was previously.

Chant the following at any time, either out loud or silently:

O Goddess,
I need your grace
To replenish my aura which has diminished in space
Hear my Plea
So mote it be!

Spell to Create a Wand

You will need:

Access to an oak tree
A stone or crystal you found yourself
Full Moon
Knife
Strong glue that has been energized

Instructions:

On a full moon night, go to the oak tree. Find a branch either on the ground below it, or one still on the tree that you can easily reach.

Approach the trunk of the tree and hug it while saying:

O Mighty Oak, I ask you to hear
My request to have a branch that is near

If you feel good about continuing to take a branch, do so. If you feel any negativity you should leave.

Cut a branch from the tree, with the length you desire. Around 12 inches is recommended.

Sit under the tree and hollow out one end of the branch for your stone or crystal.

Glue the stone or crystal to the end of the branch.

Go out from under the tree and select a safe place to leave your wand outside over night. This will allow the power of the moon to infuse it and the glue to harden.

The next day return for your wand. You may carve or paint the wand if you choose.

Spell to Enchant and Bless Your Herb Garden

You will need:

4 moss agate stones
Morning

Instructions:

On any morning take the stones out to your garden. Go to any corner and place one stone on the ground saying:

With this stone one my planting is done

Now go to the next corner and place one stone on the ground saying:

With this stone two I bless all morning dew

Now go to the next corner and place one stone on the ground saying:

With this stone three negativity will flee

Now go to the last corner and place one stone on the ground saying:

With this stone four the garden is cared for

Leave the stones where they are as long as you have a garden within their lines.

Spell to Consecrate a Book

You will need:

Book to be enchanted
Energized pen

Instructions:

Place the book in front of you and both your hands on it. Close your eyes and meditate until you feel calm and peaceful.

Open the book and draw a pentacle in its front cover.

Write your name beneath the pentacle and say:

By the power of the sun and the moon
By the power of the Earth and sea
I consecrate this book
So mote it be

To Enchant a Written Spell

You will need:

Piece of paper
Quill or energized pen
Ink in a color that corresponds with the spell you are writing
Candle in color that corresponds with the spell you are writing

Instructions:

Light the candle and place it in front of you.

Carefully write out the spell you wish to perform.

Fold the paper in thirds and place it under the candle.

The candle should be allowed to finish and once it does your spell paper is enchanted and ready for working.

Spell to Enchant a Crystal

You will need:

Candle in a color that represents you
Crystal

Instructions:

Place the candle before you and light it.

Hold the crystal in your hands and say:

O Goddess by the light and smoke of this flame
I enchant this crystal in your name
So I will it
So mote it be

Now pass the crystal through the candle flame, place it at the base of the candle, and allow the candle to finish.

When the candle is done, the crystal is enchanted and ready for you.

You can charge several crystals at a time this way.

Spell to Consecrate Water

<u>You will need</u>:

3 teaspoons of sea salt
Glass bottle with cork or other seal
Boiled water

<u>Instructions</u>:

Start by boiling your glass bottle and the water you wish to consecrate for 3 minutes.

Add the boiled water to the bottle and go outside in direct sunlight or moonlight.

Add the salt to the water and shake the bottle to dissolve the salt.

Leave the bottle outside for a full 24 hours with the lid loosely secured.

After 24 hours, the water is done and should be stored in a cool dark place when not in use. The consecrated water is good for a full moon cycle and then should be replaced.

Spell to Bless a Pen

<u>You will need</u>:

New pen
Strand of your hair
Sunlight

<u>Instructions</u>:

Take the strand of hair and tie it around the pen if possible. If impossible, lay the strand across the pen.

Place the pen in sunlight and say:

Bless this pen with sunlight
To serve me right
And to serve only me
So mote it be

The pen should be left in sunlight for 3 hours.

Spell to Enchant a Dagger

You will need:

New dagger
White candle
Red candle
Silver candle
Green candle
Blue candle
Salt
Bowl of consecrated water
Altar

Instructions:

Make a pentacle in salt on your altar.

Place the white candle at the top point, the red candle at the right point, the silver candle at the bottom right point, the green candle at the bottom left point, and the blue candle at the left point.

Light the candles in the same order as you put them in place.

Wash the dagger in the consecrated water and place it in the center of the pentacle. Say the following:

Elemental forces far and wide
Imbue this dagger with your powers inside
So it harm none
The enchant be done
So I will it
So mote it be

Pass the dagger through the flames of the candles and then replace it inside the pentacle. When the candles are finished the enchantment is complete.

Charm to Protect Your Child

You will need:

White cloth
Strand of your hair
Strand of the other parent's hair (if unavailable, grandparent's hair)
Picture of your child
Pinch of salt
Black thread or ribbon

Instructions:

Spread out the white cloth before you and add the hairs, the picture, and the pinch of salt.

Draw up to corners together and as you do so visualize your arms enfolding the child and protecting them, even when you are not physically there. Tie the cloth together. Say the following:

O Child surrounded by my arms
I will always protect you from harm
So I will it
So mote it be

The charm should be kept in your child's room in a safe place.

Protection Charm

You will need:

White candle
Red candle
Piece of paper
Red ribbon
Olive oil

Instructions:

Place the red candle on the left of the white candle and light both.

With your finger, trace a pentacle on the paper using olive oil.

Roll up the paper and tie it with the ribbon. Then say the following:

I consecrate this scroll with fire
So that I may defend myself and keep my powers

Pass the rolled paper through the flame of the red candle. Then say:

I consecrate this scroll with air
So that I may defend myself and keep my powers

Now pass the rolled paper through the smoke of the white candle.

Seal the top end of the paper with red wax and the bottom end of the paper with white wax.

This charm is now complete and should be kept in a cool, dark place.

Animal Protection Spell

You will need:

2 green candles
1 gold candle
Picture or figurine to represent the animal
Consecrated salt
Consecrated water

Instructions:

The two green candles should be placed on the left. Light all of the candles.

Place the picture of the pet under the gold candle, or the figurine directly in front of it. Say the following:

Spirit of the flame burning bright
I call upon you this night

Cast your protection
And give me direction

To care for this (type of animal)
To the best of my ability

Allow the candles to finish. The picture or figurine should be kept on your altar or in another safe place.

Chant to Protect Against Worries

At any time you feel worried or afraid, chant the following as many times as necessary:

By the fire of my will
As I sit still
Protect my body, my mind, and my soul
Over which only I have control

Daily Protection Chant

This chant should be repeated three times each morning as you are getting ready to begin your day. It will provide protection throughout the day.

Elements of Sun, elements of Day
I call upon thee to protect me
So I will it, so it shall be

Made in the USA
San Bernardino, CA
08 September 2014